N
SCOTIA
TRAVEL GUIDE
2023

The Most Recent Pocket Guide to Discover Canada's Stunning

Maritime province, Featuring many insiders Tips, Unforgettable

Experiences and Hidden Treasure

EDWARD FIELD

Nova Scotia Travel Guide 2023

COPYRIGHT @ 2023 by Edward Field

TABLE OF CONTENTS

CHAPTER THREE

CHAPTER FOUR

CHPATER ELEVEN

Shopping and Souvenirs

Nova Scotian Products

Artisan Boutiques

Ideas for Unique Scotian Souvenirs

CHAPTER TWELVE

Practical Information

Currency and Banking information
Health and Safety Tips

CONCLUSION

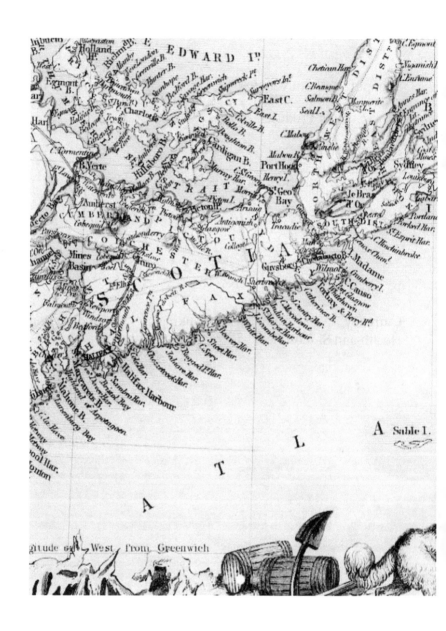

NOVA SCOTIA'S MAP

INTRODUCTION

Welcome to Nova Scotia, a province as captivating as it is diverse, where every corner tells a story, and every vista is a masterpiece. Nestled on the eastern coast of Canada, Nova Scotia beckons with its maritime charm, a place where history, culture, and breathtaking natural beauty merge into an unforgettable tapestry.

Nova Scotia, often called "New Scotland," is a place where the past whispers in the wind through the age-old lighthouses that dot its rugged coastline and the cobbled streets of its historic towns. Yet, it's also a province that looks boldly to the future, embracing innovation while preserving its rich heritage.

Here, you'll find yourself immersed in a world of pristine beaches that stretch as far as the eye can see, surrounded by the rhythm of crashing waves. As you explore the rolling landscapes and lush valleys, you'll discover vineyards that produce world-class wines, and fishing villages where lobster boils are a time-honored tradition.

Nova Scotia is an open invitation to adventure, where hiking trails wind through ancient forests and kayaking routes reveal hidden coves. It's a province that knows how to celebrate, with festivals that range from lively Celtic music gatherings to epic seafood feasts.

Whether you're drawn by the call of the sea, the warmth of its people, or the vibrant culture that pulses through its communities, Nova Scotia promises a journey filled with moments that will stay with you forever. So, step ashore, breathe in the salt-tinged air, and let Nova Scotia's welcoming embrace captivate your heart.

As of 2023, Nova Scotia is still growing and providing Visitors with exciting new experiences. You will find the following initiatives and attractions right now:

Outdoor Activities: Nova Scotia is known for its stunning natural beauty, and outdoor activities such as hiking, kayaking, and whale watching are popular in 2023. The province continued to promote its scenic trails and coastal experiences.

Culinary Tourism: Nova Scotia's culinary scene has been growing, with a focus on locally sourced and seafood-based dishes. In 2023, you could explore various food festivals and culinary tours that showcased the region's delicious offerings.

Wine and Craft Beer: Nova Scotia's wine and craft beer industry has been gaining recognition. You could visit wineries and breweries in regions like the Annapolis Valley and Wolfville to sample local beverages.

Cultural Events: Nova Scotia has a rich cultural heritage. In 2023, there are cultural events and festivals celebrating music, art, and history. These events often featured local talent.

Nova Scotia's Coastal Beauty: The province's coastline, including the iconic Cabot Trail, continued to attract visitors in 2023. Exploring coastal villages and taking in breathtaking views remained a highlight.

Heritage Sites: Nova Scotia is steeped in history, and there are many heritage sites and museums to explore. In 2023, you could learn about the region's Indigenous history, early settlers, and maritime heritage.

Lighthouses: Nova Scotia is home to numerous picturesque lighthouses. Visitors could explore these historic structures and enjoy scenic views along the coast. I have compiled intriguing sites to visit, so you can add them to your to-do list while you are there and when you return. Whether you want to hit the top photo spots or just meander around Nova Scotia exploring, you should do so.

CHAPTER ONE

Overview of Nova Scotia

History of Nova Scotia

Nova Scotia, meaning "New Scotland" in Latin, is a Canadian province steeped in history. Its story dates back centuries, and understanding its past is essential to appreciating its present. Here's a glimpse into the rich history of Nova Scotia:

Indigenous Peoples

The history of Nova Scotia begins with its Indigenous peoples, notably the Mi'kmaq, who have inhabited the region for thousands of years. They were skilled hunters, gatherers, and fishermen who developed a deep connection with the land and sea.

European Exploration

In the early 16th century, European explorers like John Cabot and Giovanni da Verrazzano sailed along the Nova Scotia coast. However, it was the arrival of Samuel de Champlain in 1605 that marked the establishment of the first European settlement, Port Royal, in what is now Annapolis Royal.

Colonial Struggles

Throughout the 17th and 18th centuries, Nova Scotia was a battleground in the struggle between the British and the French for North American dominance. The Treaty of Utrecht in 1713 officially ceded Nova Scotia to the British, setting the stage for further conflicts.

Acadian Expulsion

One of the most tragic episodes in Nova Scotia's history was the Acadian Expulsion (1755-1764). The British forcibly removed the Acadian population, resulting in immense suffering and the loss of cultural heritage.

American Revolution

During the American Revolution, Nova Scotia became a haven for Loyalists fleeing the newly formed United States. Their arrival significantly influenced the province's demographics and culture.

Confederation

Nova Scotia played a pivotal role in the Confederation of Canada in 1867, becoming one of its founding provinces. This decision marked a significant turning point in its history.

Modern Era

In the 20th century, Nova Scotia's economy evolved from a reliance on natural resources to include sectors like manufacturing, technology, and tourism. It has become known for its friendly people, strong communities, and stunning landscapes.

Nova Scotian Culture

Nova Scotia's culture is a tapestry woven with threads from its Indigenous roots, European heritage, and the influence of immigrants from around the world. Key aspects of Nova Scotian culture include:

Music and Dance

Music is deeply ingrained in Nova Scotia's culture. Celtic traditions, influenced by Scottish and Irish immigrants, are particularly strong. Fiddle music and lively ceilidhs (social gatherings with music and dance) are popular. Acadian and Mi'kmaq musical traditions also enrich the cultural landscape.

Cuisine

Nova Scotia's cuisine reflects its maritime location. Seafood is a staple, with lobster, scallops, and Digby clams as local delicacies. Don't forget to try a "lobster boil" or enjoy a hearty bowl of seafood chowder.

Festivals

The province hosts numerous festivals celebrating its culture, music, and heritage. The Celtic Colours International Festival and the Stan Rogers Folk Festival are highlights for music enthusiasts. The Nova Scotia Multicultural Festival showcases the province's diversity.

Visual Arts and Crafts

Nova Scotia boasts a thriving arts scene. You'll find art galleries featuring local talent, and artisan communities on Cape Breton Island where traditional crafts like rug hooking and pottery are practiced.

Nova Scotia Geography

Nova Scotia is located on the eastern coast of Canada and is part of the Maritime region. Its geography is diverse and captivating:

Coastal Beauty

Nova Scotia is known for its rugged coastline, with picturesque fishing villages, cliffs, and countless bays and inlets. The Bay of Fundy, famous for its extreme tides, is a natural wonder.

Cape Breton Island

Connected to the mainland by a causeway, Cape Breton Island is renowned for its dramatic landscapes, including the Cape Breton Highlands and the Cabot Trail.

Lakes and Rivers

Inland, Nova Scotia is dotted with lakes and rivers, making it a haven for outdoor enthusiasts. Kejimkujik National Park is a prime example of the province's natural beauty.

Nova Scotia Climate

The climate in Nova Scotia varies from region to region:

Coastal Influence

Coastal areas experience milder temperatures due to the moderating effect of the Atlantic Ocean. Summers are pleasant, and winters are relatively mild, with less snowfall than inland areas.

Inland and Highland Regions

Inland and highland regions, like Cape Breton, tend to have more variable weather. Winters can be colder, and snowfall is more significant, making these areas ideal for winter sports enthusiasts.

Nova Scotia Language

English is the predominant language spoken in Nova Scotia, with the majority of residents speaking it fluently. However, you may also hear French, especially in Acadian communities, and Mi'kmaq, the language of the Indigenous Mi'kmaq people. Nova Scotia's linguistic diversity reflects its multicultural heritage.

I've provided an overview of Nova Scotia, delving into its history, culture, geography, climate, and language. This foundation sets the stage for a deeper exploration of this enchanting province.

CHAPTER TWO

Planning Your Trip to Nova Scotia

W hen planning a trip to Nova Scotia, it's important to consider several key factors, including the best time to visit, entry requirements, and transportation options. Let's explore each of these aspects to help you plan your Nova Scotia adventure.

Best Time to Visit

Summer (June to August): This is the most popular time to visit Nova Scotia. The weather is warm, with average temperatures ranging from 15°C to 25°C (59°F to 77°F). Summer offers the best conditions for outdoor activities, festivals, and exploring the stunning coastline. Be prepared for larger crowds and higher accommodation prices, especially in tourist hotspots like Halifax and Cape Breton.

Fall (September to November): Fall in Nova Scotia is a breathtaking spectacle as the foliage bursts into vibrant shades of red, orange, and yellow. The weather remains pleasant, with cooler temperatures than summer. This is an excellent time for hiking and enjoying cultural festivals, such as the Celtic Colours International Festival on Cape Breton Island.

Spring (April to June): Spring is a quieter time to visit Nova Scotia. While temperatures can still be chilly, you'll avoid the summer crowds. Spring is also a great season for viewing wildlife and enjoying the early blooms of flowers and trees.

Winter (December to March): If you're a fan of winter sports like skiing and snowshoeing, or if you want to experience a cozy holiday season, consider visiting Nova Scotia in winter. Coastal areas have milder winters than inland regions, and you can enjoy winter festivals and activities.

Visa Requirements:

Citizens of the United States do not need a visa for short tourist visits (up to 6 months).

Citizens of other countries may require a visitor visa or an Electronic Travel Authorization (eTA) to enter Canada. For the most recent visa requirements, visit the Government of Canada's official website.

Passport:

To enter Canada, all visitors, including U.S. citizens, require a current passport.

Check the most recent COVID-19 entry requirements and travel warnings. Testing, quarantine, and vaccinations may be necessary conditions.

Customs Regulations:

Familiarize yourself with Canadian customs regulations regarding items you can bring into the country and declare at the border.

Transportation Options

Air Travel:

The Halifax Stanfield International Airport (YHZ) is the largest airport in Nova Scotia and serves as the primary gateway for international travelers. It's well-connected to major Canadian and international cities.

Ground Transportation:

Car Rentals: Renting a car is a popular option for exploring Nova Scotia, especially if you plan to venture into rural areas. Major car rental agencies operate at the airport and in Halifax.

Public Transportation: Halifax has a reliable public bus system, and there are intercity bus services connecting major towns and cities. Via Rail offers passenger train services between Halifax and other Canadian cities.

Ferries: Ferries are a unique way to explore Nova Scotia's coastal regions, including routes to Cape Breton Island and Digby Neck.

Local Transportation:

In cities like Halifax, you can get around using buses, ferries, and taxis. Halifax also has bike-sharing programs and pedestrian-friendly areas.

Roadways:

Nova Scotia has a well-maintained road network, and driving is generally safe. Always keep to the right side of the road when driving.

Planning your trip to Nova Scotia involves careful consideration of the best time to visit, entry requirements, and transportation options. Once you've covered these essentials, you can focus on crafting an itinerary that allows you to experience the province's natural beauty, culture, and history to the fullest.

CHAPTER THREE

Getting To Nova Scotia

Travelers find Nova Scotia to be an intriguing location because of its untamed coastline, charming history, and dynamic culture. Getting to Nova Scotia is the first step in your journey to discover this marine treasure, regardless of whether you're taking a flight from afar or setting off on a road trip adventure. We'll look at all the different ways to get to Nova Scotia in this chapter, including airports, airlines, roads, and nautical possibilities.

Maritime Airports and Airlines

The main entry point into Nova Scotia is Halifax Stanfield International Airport (YHZ), which is situated about 35 kilometers (22 miles) north of the city center of Halifax. With both domestic and foreign flights, it is the busiest airport in the Atlantic Canada region. To ensure that your arrival and departure are comfortable, the airport provides a wide range of services and amenities.

Airports Halifax Stanfield are served by airlines

Halifax Stanfield International Airport hosts a number of significant airlines that offer both domestic and international connections. Among these airlines are:

From Halifax, Air Canada, the nation's flag carrier, operates a large number of domestic and international routes.

Another well-known Canadian airline, WestJet, operates flights from Halifax to a number of locations in both Canada and the US.

Porter Airlines: This airline, which is renowned for providing excellent service, operates flights from Halifax to destinations such as Toronto and Ottawa.

Delta Air Lines: Offers simple connectivity to destinations within the US and abroad.

United Airlines: Provides routes to the United States, making it simple to connect to other countries.

Air Transat is a well-liked option for visitors looking for transatlantic adventures because of its seasonal focus on flights to European locations.

Other Airports in Nova Scotia

Nova Scotia features a number of minor airports that service smaller towns and provide domestic connections, even though Halifax Stanfield International Airport serves as the main entry point. These airports include, among others:

Sydney/J.A. Douglas McCurdy Airport (YQY) is a Cape Breton Island airport that provides service to the area and connects to Halifax and Toronto.

Yarmouth International Airport (YQI), which serves southwest Nova Scotia, with connections to Portland, Maine and Halifax.

Charlottetown Airport (YYG): Although in Prince Edward Island, this airport is a convenient option for travelers to western Nova Scotia.

Road Routes Trip

For those who prefer the scenic route, Nova Scotia is accessible by road from various locations. Here are some key road routes to consider:

From New Brunswick

Trans-Canada Highway (Route 104): You can travel into Nova Scotia on the Trans-Canada Highway (Route 104) if you're traveling from New Brunswick or another region of

Canada. The scenery along this road, both rural and coastal, is spectacular.

From Maine, USA

Driving from the United States, you can enter Nova Scotia from Maine via Interstate 95 and Route 1. To get to Houlton, Maine, take Interstate 95, then take Route 1 to the New Brunswick side of the border. You can then join Route 2 of the Trans-Canada Highway to travel into Nova Scotia from there.

Confederation Bridge from Prince Edward Island: The beautiful Confederation Bridge joins Borden-Carleton, PEI, and Cape Jourimain, New Brunswick, making it possible for visitors from Prince Edward Island to reach Nova Scotia. Follow Route 16 into Nova Scotia from there.

Nova Scotia's maritime heritage extends to its diverse travel options, including ferries and cruises.

Ferries

Bay Ferries: Bay Ferries operates several routes between Nova Scotia and neighboring provinces. The most famous is the ferry between Yarmouth, Nova Scotia, and Portland, Maine, offering a scenic and convenient way to explore both the Maritimes and New England.

Northumberland Ferries: This company connects Nova Scotia with Prince Edward Island via the ferry route between Wood Islands, PEI, and Caribou, Nova Scotia. It's a great option for exploring both provinces.

Cruises

Cruise Ports: Nova Scotia is a popular destination for cruise ships. Ports of call include Halifax, Sydney, and Yarmouth, among others. Cruise passengers can explore the province's attractions and experience its rich culture during their shore excursions.

Small Ship Cruises: For a more intimate maritime experience, consider booking a small ship cruise. These cruises often explore less-visited coastal areas, providing a unique perspective of Nova Scotia's natural beauty.

The fun aspect of your trip to this interesting province is getting to Nova Scotia. You're in for a spectacular vacation filled with breathtaking scenery, rich history, and kind hospitality whether you decide to fly into Halifax, set out on a gorgeous road trip, or discover Nova Scotia's marine connections through ferries and cruises.

CHAPTER FOUR

Top Attractions in Nova Scotia

A diverse selection of attractions that appeal to all types of travelers are available in the province of Nova Scotia, which is rich in natural beauty, history, and culture. In this chapter, we'll look at a few of the top sights that you should include on your list of places to see while you go across Nova Scotia.

Halifax

Historic Downtown

Halifax Waterfront: Take a stroll along the energetic Halifax Waterfront to begin your journey of the capital city of Nova

Scotia. A lovely variety of stores, eateries, historical places, and attractions can be found here. Don't pass up the opportunity to see the Maritime Museum of the Atlantic, which houses an intriguing collection of nautical relics, including the Titanic display.

Citadel Hill is a star-shaped fortress that dominates the city's skyline and provides a window into Halifax's military past. Visitors can stroll around the ramparts, observe the Noon Gun being fired, and take in the expansive views of the city from the fort's elevated position.

Historic Properties: The Historic Properties are a group of exquisitely preserved 19th-century buildings located in the heart of Halifax. They house specialty stores, art galleries, and restaurants, making it a great location to learn about Nova Scotia's history and get one-of-a-kind gifts.

Halifax, Nova Scotia

Peggy's Cove

Peggy's Cove: This picturesque fishing village is world-renowned for its iconic lighthouse, perched atop granite rocks overlooking the Atlantic Ocean. Peggy's Cove is a photographer's dream, offering stunning coastal views and a chance to witness the rugged beauty of Nova Scotia's shoreline.

Peggy's Cove Lighthouse: The lighthouse, still in operation today, is one of the most photographed in Canada. Climb the rocks around it, explore the quaint village, and savor the freshest seafood at local restaurants.

Peggy's Cove

The Cabot Trail

The Cabot Trail: Located on Cape Breton Island, the Cabot Trail is often hailed as one of the world's most scenic drives. This winding coastal highway offers breathtaking views of the Gulf of Cape Breton Highlands, Atlantic Ocean, and St. Lawrence. Along the way, you can stop at lookouts, hike through the national park, and enjoy the vibrant fall foliage.

Cape Breton Highlands National Park: A significant portion of the Cabot Trail runs through this national park, known for its rugged cliffs, deep river canyons, and lush forests. Hiking trails of varying difficulty levels cater to all skill levels, providing opportunities to spot wildlife and enjoy the pristine natural surroundings.

Celtic Culture: Cape Breton Island is also a cultural hub known for its rich Celtic heritage. You can experience traditional music and dance at local pubs and cultural events, providing a glimpse into Nova Scotia's vibrant cultural scene.

The best things to do in Nova Scotia include Peggy's Cove and Cape Breton Island's natural wonders as well as the province's historic cityscape in Halifax. Every traveler may find something to enjoy in Nova Scotia, whether they are interested in history, outdoor activities, or simply soaking in the gorgeous environment.

Nova Scotia Travel Guide 2023   Edward Field

Cape Breton Island

Cabot Trail- Neil's Harbour

Bras d'Or Lake

The enormous and tranquil saltwater lake of Bras d'Or Lake, sometimes known as the "Inland Sea," is situated on Cape Breton Island. Boaters, kayakers, and environment lovers will find bliss in this Biosphere Reserve, which was designated by UNESCO. The calm waters of the lake are filled with islands and coves, making it the perfect place to explore by boat.

Sailing and boating: The lake is a sanctuary for sailors and boaters, and it regularly stages regattas and other activities. To really appreciate the lake's beauty and serenity, charter a sailboat or go on a guided trip.

Wildlife viewing: The region around Bras d'Or Lake is abundant with wildlife. Bald eagles, ospreys, and other ducks can all be observed by birdwatchers, and seals and porpoises are frequently spotted in the ocean.

Lunenburg

A charming hamlet on Nova Scotia's South Shore, Lunenburg is one of the best-preserved examples of a British colonial settlement in North America and is listed on the UNESCO World Heritage List.

History and architecture: The town is renowned for its small streets and colorful, old buildings. Discover the Bluenose II schooner, the Fisheries Museum of the Atlantic, and the town's seafaring heritage.

Waterfront: Lunenburg's waterfront is a bustling area with restaurants, galleries, and shops. Enjoy fresh seafood while overlooking the harbor or take a boat tour to appreciate the town's coastal beauty.

A taste of Nova Scotia cuisine at Lunenburg

Annapolis Valley

Annapolis Valley: This fertile valley in western Nova Scotia is known as the province's fruit basket. It's a region of rolling hills, picturesque farms, and charming towns.

Wine and Cider Tours: Annapolis Valley is famous for its wineries and cideries. Take a tour to sample locally produced wines, ciders, and artisanal cheeses.

Historic Sites: Explore historic sites like Port-Royal National Historic Site and Fort Anne National Historic Site to learn about the area's early French and British colonial history.

Louisbourg Fortress

Louisbourg Fortress: Located on Cape Breton Island, the Louisbourg Fortress is a meticulously reconstructed 18th-century French fortress. It provides a fascinating glimpse into colonial life in the 1700s.

Living History: Interact with costumed interpreters as they go about daily tasks, and witness historic reenactments that bring this era to life.

Scenic Beauty: The fortress overlooks the Atlantic Ocean and offers spectacular views. Explore the nearby fishing village of Louisbourg for a taste of local maritime culture.

Vineyards and wineries

Vineyards and wineries: Nova Scotia's environment is perfect for growing cool-climate grapes like Chardonnay and Riesling, which make for high-quality wines. Numerous wineries and vineyards can be found in the province, and many of them provide tours and tastings.

Try the distinctive wine of Nova Scotia, Tidal Bay, a crisp and fragrant white wine that goes great with seafood.

Tours that are scenic: Winery tours frequently take you through lovely vineyards with views of the ocean and rolling hills.

There is something for everyone in this maritime province thanks to Nova Scotia's diverse attractions, which range from the serene beauty of Bras d'Or Lake to the historic charm of Lunenburg, the agricultural bounty of Annapolis Valley, the immersive experience at Louisbourg Fortress, and the burgeoning wine industry. Exploring these attractions will make your Nova Scotia journey unforgettable.

Grand Pré National Historic Site: The Grand Pré National Historic Site, a UNESCO World Heritage Site, honors the terrible history of the Acadian people and is located in the **Annapolis Valley**. It details how the British drove the Acadians out of Canada in the 18th century.

Visitor Center: The location has a visitor center with educational exhibits and displays that provide light on the Acadian people's history, culture, and sufferings during the deportation.

Grand Pré is especially well-known for its magnificent gardens, which combine French and Acadian horticultural traditions. The grounds offer a tranquil setting for contemplation and appreciating the local culture.

UNESCO World Heritage Site

UNESCO World Heritage Site: Lunenburg and the Grand Pré National Historic Site are just two of the UNESCO World Heritage Sites in Nova Scotia. The great cultural and historical significance of the province on a global scale is highlighted by these distinctions.

Outstanding global significance: Nova Scotia's UNESCO World history Sites are acknowledged for their exceptional global significance, reflecting natural and cultural history that merits preservation and protection.

The Lighthouse at Cape Forchu

The Cape Forchu Lighthouse is a well-known nautical landmark and is situated close to Yarmouth on Nova Scotia's southwest coast. Anyone visiting the province's shore should make sure to stop at the lighthouse and take in the beautiful surroundings.

Views: The rocky coastlines, Atlantic Ocean, and jagged shoreline are all breathtakingly visible from Cape Forchu. An wonderful vantage point for taking in the breathtaking coastline view is the lighthouse itself.

Visitor Center: There is a visitor center on the property where you can find out more about the history of the lighthouse and the area's maritime heritage.

Fisheries Museum of the Atlantic

The Fisheries Museum of the Atlantic is a museum devoted to conserving and promoting Nova Scotia's rich nautical legacy. It is situated on the city's picturesque waterfront.

The museum has a wide variety of exhibits, including fishing gear, model ships, and historical accounts of the local fishing business.

Bluenose II, a renowned schooner famed for its racing skills, is also housed at the museum. The ship may be explored by guests, who can also discover its fascinating past.

These landmarks provide fascinating perspectives on the natural splendor, maritime history, and cultural heritage of Nova Scotia. From Cape Forchu's stunning scenery to the Fisheries Museum of the Atlantic's maritime traditions to the heartbreaking history of Grand Pré, each site adds to the rich tapestry of experiences awaiting travelers in this beautiful province.

CHAPTER FIVE

Outdoor Activities in Nova Scotia

The varied scenery of Nova Scotia, which is characterized by rocky beaches, lush forests, and immaculate lakes, offers the ideal setting for a variety of outdoor activities. We'll look at some of the best outdoor pursuits that nature lovers and thrill seekers may partake in in this seaside region in this chapter.

Coastal Trail at Cape Chignecto

Cumberland County's Cape Chignecto Coastal Trail offers a strenuous and breathtaking journey along the Bay of Fundy, which is renowned for having the highest tides in the world. The trail offers options for multi-day backpacking excursions as it meanders through lush forests, rugged cliffs, and immaculate beaches.

Highlands of Cape Breton National Park

Highlands of Cape Breton National Park: There are a variety of hiking paths in this national park on Cape Breton Island to suit all skill levels. Visit the Skyline Trail, which offers sweeping views of the Gulf of St. Lawrence.

Kejimkujik National Park

Kejimkujik National Park: Situated in the southwest of Nova Scotia, Kejimkujik provides chances for both kayaking and hiking. The park's wide route network leads

National Park of Kejimkujik

Kejimkujik National Park is a paddling lover's dream. It has serene, connected lakes and rivers that are great for canoeing and kayaking. To explore the park's waterways, you can either rent equipment or sign up for a trip.

Kejimkujik National Park Seaside

Eastern Shore

Eastern Shore: The Tangier River and the Musquodoboit River are just two of the many paddling options available in the Eastern Shore area of Nova Scotia. The peaceful estuaries and animal viewing in this area are well-known.

Playing at Cabot Links

Cabot Links is one of Canada's top golf courses, and it is situated near Inverness on Cape Breton Island. With beautiful ocean views from every hole, it provides an amazing golfing experience by the sea.

Scottish Links

Highlands Links: Another golf course on Cape Breton Island, Highlands Links is renowned for its difficult design and picturesque location inside Cape Breton Highlands National Park.

The Bay of Fundy is a popular spot for whale viewing and is known for its abundant marine biodiversity. It is situated between Nova Scotia and New Brunswick. Humpback whales, minke whales, and even the threatened North Atlantic right whale can all be seen.

Island Brier

Brier Island: This island is frequently cited as one of Nova Scotia's top spots for whale watching. Tours leave from this location to see the whales as they forage in the Gulf of Maine's nutrient-rich waters. Nova Scotia offers an array of outdoor activities that allow you to immerse yourself in the province's natural beauty and adventure. Whatever your outdoor passion, Nova Scotia has an experience waiting for you.

CHAPTER SIX

Cultural Experiences in Nova Scotia

The vibrant traditions and diversified histories of Nova Scotia's inhabitants are reflected in the province's rich cultural tapestry. We'll look at a few of the cultural experiences that visitors to this alluring province can expect in this chapter.

Celtic Music: The province of Nova Scotia has strong ties to the Celtic people, and Celtic music is a significant component of its cultural legacy. Visit neighborhood pubs and festivals for entertaining performances of fiddles, bagpipes, and traditional tunes. The Scottish and Irish influences on the history of the area are reflected in the music.

Celtic Festivals

Celtic Festivals: To honor the province's Celtic ancestry, Nova Scotia celebrates a number of Celtic festivals throughout the year. A highlight is the Celtic Colours International Festival on Cape Breton Island, which features top-notch artists and exciting cultural events.

Scottish Games

Experience the thrill of age-old Scottish contests like caber tossing and hammer throwing during Highland Games celebrations in Nova Scotia. These celebrations of Scottish culture frequently feature upbeat musical and dancing performances.

Studios and galleries for art

Toronto Art Scene

The capital city of Halifax is home to a bustling arts scene, with several galleries and studios showing the creations of regional artists. View a varied collection of Canadian and foreign art at the Art Gallery of Nova Scotia.

Lunenburg Galleries

Lunenburg Galleries: Lunenburg, a historic town, has a thriving artistic community. Explore art galleries filled with the creations of outstanding painters, sculptors, and makers.

You might come across the ideal work of art to remember your journey.

The Creative Hub of Cape Breton

The Creative Hub of Cape Breton: On Cape Breton Island, artisans and artists produce a wide range of works, including ceramics, jewelry, textiles, and folk art. Visit art galleries and craft stores to see the creative process in action and to buy one-of-a-kind, handcrafted mementos.

Nova Scotia's cultural experiences provide a window into the province's rich heritage and the talents of its people. From the lively sounds of Celtic music and the excitement of Highland Games to the inspiring works of local artists in galleries and studios, you'll find a wealth of cultural treasures waiting to be discovered during your travels in Nova Scotia.

CHAPTER SEVEN

Cuisine Delight in Nova Scotia

The culinary scene of Nova Scotia is a delicious fusion of local products, fresh seafood, and a long marine culture. We'll look at the culinary treats Nova Scotia has to offer foodies in this chapter.

Seafood-based dishes

Nova Scotia is well known for its succulent lobster, which is regarded as some of the best in the world. You must try lobster rolls, lobster chowder, and plain cooked lobster with butter.

Menu at Birch and Anchor- One of Halifax's biggest

ocean front garden

Nova Scotia Travel Guide 2023   Edward Field

Salt Cod Fritters menu at Lunenburg

(Nova Scotia salt, cod, Yukon Gold potato, garlic, parsley,

spicy honey, fresh mint)

Dungeness crabs

Digby Scallops: The sweet, soft scallops from Digby, on the Bay of Fundy, are world-famous. They go well with pan-seared dishes, chowder, and seafood platters.

Smoked Mackerel

Smoked Mackerel: Smoked mackerel is a popular local delicacy. The smoky flavor pairs wonderfully with crackers or in salads.

Fish and Chips

Fish and Chips: You'll find excellent fish and chips throughout Nova Scotia. Enjoy crispy, golden-fried fish, often accompanied by fresh-cut fries and tartar sauce.

Nova Scotia Oysters

Nova Scotia Oysters: The province's coastal waters are home to an abundance of oyster beds. These oysters are often enjoyed raw, with a dash of lemon or mignonette sauce, offering a taste of the ocean's briny goodness.

Farmer's Markets

Market at Halifax Seaport

One of the oldest markets in North America is the Halifax Seaport Farmers' Market, which is situated on the water. It provides a wide selection of local vendors' fresh vegetables, artisanal goods, baked goods, and crafts. It's a fantastic location for discovering the local cuisine scene and finding one-of-a-kind gifts.

Market for Farmers in Wolfville

Wolfville Farmers' Market: This market, which is situated in the heart of the Annapolis Valley, highlights the wealth of the area's agriculture. Fresh fruits, veggies, cheeses, wines, and much more are available.

Market for Farmers in Lunenburg

The lovely village of Lunenburg is home to the Lunenburg Farmers' Market, which is a terrific opportunity to try out local fare including shellfish, artisanal cheeses, and handcrafted goods.

Local Food Festivals

Nova Scotia Lobster Crawl

The Nova Scotia Lobster Crawl, which takes place in February when lobster is at its peak, is a celebration that honors all things lobster. Take part in lobster tastings, gastronomic events, and even an art crawl with a lobster theme.

Icewine Festival in Nova Scotia

The Nova Scotia Icewine Festival is a celebration of the region's ice wines and is held in the center of the Annapolis Valley. While tasting several ice wines, you can discover how wine is made.

Devour! Food Film Festival

Devour! The cuisine movies Fest is a distinctive event that brings together cuisine and movies in Wolfville. Enjoy culinary classes, celebrity chef dinners, and film screenings about food.

The culinary sector in Nova Scotia is a true representation of the province's maritime heritage and dedication to using local, seasonal foods. Whether you're savoring succulent seafood, exploring vibrant farmers' markets, or indulging in the festivities of local food festivals, you'll discover a world of delicious flavors and culinary delights during your travels in Nova Scotia.

CHAPTER EIGHT

Beaches and Coastal Escapes in Nova Scotia

With its pristine beaches, breathtaking coastal drives, and tranquil seaside camps and retreats, Nova Scotia's coastline is a veritable treasure trove of natural beauty. We'll look at the coastal delights that make Nova Scotia the ideal vacation spot for beachgoers and people looking for a peaceful seaside getaway in this chapter.

Beaches in Nova Scotia

Lawrencetown Beach: Located just outside of Halifax on the Eastern Shore, Lawrencetown Beach is famous for its excellent surfing conditions. Whether you're a seasoned surfer or a novice looking to try, this beach offers an invigorating experience.

Lawrencetown Beach

Crystal Crescent Beach: This crescent-shaped beach, also near Halifax, is known for its crystal-clear waters and white sandy shores. It's a popular spot for swimming, picnicking, and exploring the nearby hiking trails.

Crystal Crescent Beach

Crystal Crescent Beach

Ingonish Beach: Part of Cape Breton Highlands National Park, Ingonish Beach is a picturesque sandy oasis surrounded by rolling hills and the rugged beauty of the Cabot Trail. It's an ideal spot for beachcombing and enjoying the Atlantic's cool waters.

Martinique Beach: Located on the Eastern Shore, Martinique Beach is known for its vast sandy shores and towering dunes. It's one of the longest sandy beaches in the province, making it perfect for long walks and beachcombing.

Coastal Drives

Cabot Trail: The Cabot Trail is one of Canada's most iconic coastal drives, offering breathtaking views of the Gulf of St. Lawrence and the Atlantic Ocean. The route takes you through Cape Breton Highlands National Park, where you can stop at lookouts and hike along the dramatic cliffs.

The Cabot Trail

Lighthouse Route: This scenic drive along the South Shore takes you past charming fishing villages, rugged coastlines, and, as the name suggests, numerous lighthouses. It's a picturesque journey through Nova Scotia's maritime heritage.

Sunrise Trail: Located along the Northumberland Shore, the Sunrise Trail is known for its stunning sunrises and tranquil beaches. It's a less-traveled route that leads you to hidden gems and peaceful coastal escapes.

Seaside Camps and Retreats

Kejimkujik Seaside: Part of Kejimkujik National Park, this seaside area offers camping and hiking opportunities along pristine coastal landscapes. Campers can fall asleep to the soothing sound of the waves.

Cape Breton Island Retreats: Cape Breton offers a range of seaside retreats, from cozy cabins to luxurious beachfront accommodations. Enjoy tranquil mornings and spectacular sunsets by the sea.

White Point Beach Resort: Located on Nova Scotia's South Shore, this beachfront resort offers a variety of accommodations, including cottages and chalets. It's a peaceful place to unwind and savor the coastal ambiance.

Nova Scotia's beaches, coastal drives, and seaside camps and retreats provide the perfect setting for relaxation and rejuvenation. Whether you're seeking the thrill of surfing, the tranquility of a coastal drive, or the serenity of a seaside campsite, Nova Scotia's coastline has something to offer every traveler looking for a coastal escape.

CHAPTER NINE

Lighthouse Tour in Nova Scotia

Nova Scotia's rugged coastline is dotted with iconic lighthouses, each with its own unique charm and maritime history. In this chapter, we'll embark on a lighthouse tour, exploring some of the most iconic and picturesque lighthouses that grace the shores of Nova Scotia.

Peggy's Cove Lighthouse: Perhaps the most famous lighthouse in Nova Scotia, Peggy's Cove Lighthouse stands atop granite rocks overlooking the Atlantic Ocean. Its iconic red-and-white exterior against the backdrop of the rocky coastline is a photographer's dream.

Cape Forchu Lighthouse: Located near Yarmouth on the southwestern tip of Nova Scotia, the Cape Forchu Lighthouse is known for its unique "apple core" shape. It offers breathtaking views of the rugged coastline and the Bay of Fundy.

Louisbourg Lighthouse: This historic lighthouse on Cape Breton Island marks the entrance to Louisbourg Harbor. It's situated near the impressive Fortress of Louisbourg, adding to the charm of the area.

Sambro Island Lighthouse: As the oldest operational lighthouse in the Americas, Sambro Island Lighthouse has been guiding ships into Halifax Harbor since 1758. Located on a small island, it offers a fascinating glimpse into maritime history.

Cape George Lighthouse: Perched on a bluff overlooking the Northumberland Strait, the Cape George Lighthouse provides stunning views of the strait and Prince Edward Island. It's a tranquil spot to take in the serene coastal landscape.

Cape d'Or Lighthouse: Located on the Bay of Fundy, the Cape d'Or Lighthouse offers dramatic views of the highest tides in the world. The rugged coastline and nearby sea caves make this a captivating destination for nature lovers.

Pictou Lighthouse: This charming lighthouse stands at the entrance to Pictou Harbor. The town of Pictou is known as the "Birthplace of New Scotland," and the lighthouse adds to the area's maritime character.

The Lighthouse Route: Nova Scotia's South Shore is known for its scenic Lighthouse Route. This coastal drive takes you past numerous lighthouses, offering opportunities to stop and explore these maritime landmarks.

Many tour operators in Nova Scotia offer guided tours focused on lighthouses. These tours provide historical context, access to remote lighthouses, and the chance to learn about the keepers who tended to them.

Nova Scotia's lighthouses not only serve as navigational aids but also as symbols of the province's rich maritime heritage. As you embark on your lighthouse tour, you'll discover the rugged beauty, historical significance, and coastal charm that make these iconic beacons an integral part of Nova Scotia's landscape.

CHAPTER TEN

Family-Friendly Activities in Nova Scotia

Nova Scotia, with its stunning landscapes, rich history, and welcoming communities, is a fantastic destination for families looking for memorable experiences. This chapter will guide you through some of the best family-friendly activities in the province, including visits to zoos and wildlife parks. Whether you're exploring the vibrant city of Halifax or venturing into the picturesque countryside, Nova Scotia has something to offer for every member of the family.

Exploring Nova Scotia with Your Family

1. Halifax Citadel National Historic Site

Start your family adventure in the heart of Nova Scotia's capital, Halifax, at the Citadel National Historic Site. This well-preserved fortress takes you back in time to the 19th century with its costumed interpreters, cannon firings, and captivating history. Kids can participate in interactive programs and learn about the life of a soldier in the 1800s.

2. Peggy's Cove

A visit to Nova Scotia wouldn't be complete without seeing Peggy's Cove, a charming fishing village known for its iconic lighthouse perched on rugged granite shores. While the area itself is breathtaking, exploring the rocks and tide pools provides an educational experience for children interested in marine life.

3. Maritime Museum of the Atlantic

Discover the maritime heritage of Nova Scotia at the Maritime Museum of the Atlantic in Halifax. This museum showcases artifacts from the Titanic, exhibits on the Halifax Explosion, and a fascinating collection of ships and marine history. It's an engaging way for kids to learn about the province's deep ties to the sea.

4. Halifax Waterfront

Stroll along the Halifax Waterfront, where you'll find a variety of family-friendly activities. From the Discovery Centre, an interactive science museum, to the boardwalk with street performers, shops, and restaurants, there's something for everyone. Don't forget to indulge in some famous Nova Scotian seafood.

Zoos and Wildlife Parks in Nova Scotia

Nova Scotia's natural beauty extends beyond its landscapes; it's also home to a diverse range of wildlife. Exploring zoos and wildlife parks in the province offers an opportunity for children to connect with nature in a fun and educational way.

1. Shubenacadie Wildlife Park

Located just an hour from Halifax, Shubenacadie Wildlife Park is a fantastic place for families to observe native wildlife. The park is home to bears, deer, wolves, and various bird species. Kids will love the chance to learn about these animals and witness their natural behaviors.

2. Oaklawn Farm Zoo

For a more exotic animal experience, visit the Oaklawn Farm Zoo in Aylesford. This zoo boasts a wide array of animals, including lions, tigers, giraffes, and monkeys. It's not only a fun day out but also an opportunity for children to develop an appreciation for global biodiversity.

3. Hope for Wildlife Society

Nova Scotia's wildlife rehabilitation center, Hope for Wildlife, offers a unique and educational experience. This organization rescues and rehabilitates injured and orphaned animals. Visitors can learn about their conservation efforts and even meet some of the animal ambassadors during guided tours.

4. Brier Island Whale and Seabird Cruises

If your family is eager to witness marine life in its natural habitat, consider taking a whale-watching tour from Brier Island. This area is famous for its diverse marine wildlife, including humpback and minke whales, dolphins, and a variety of seabirds. It's an awe-inspiring adventure for nature enthusiasts of all ages.

You may make enduring memories while experiencing the province's rich culture and natural beauties thanks to the family-friendly activities and wildlife encounters in Nova Scotia. Your family's vacation in this stunning province will undoubtedly be full with enjoyable and instructive activities, whether you want to see historical landmarks in Halifax or get up close and personal with animals in one of the province's wildlife parks.

CHAPTER ELEVEN

Shopping and Souvenirs in Nova Scotia

When visiting Nova Scotia, you'll discover a vibrant shopping scene filled with opportunities to bring home unique souvenirs and locally crafted products. This chapter explores the best places to shop for Nova Scotian products and provides ideas for one-of-a-kind souvenirs that will forever remind you of your time in this captivating province.

1. Nova Scotian Wine and Spirits

Nova Scotia has gained recognition for its burgeoning wine and craft beer industry. The Annapolis Valley, in particular, is known for its wineries. Consider bringing home a bottle of local wine or artisanal spirits as a delightful reminder of your visit.

2. Blue Nose II Ship Models

The Bluenose II, a famous Nova Scotian schooner, is an iconic symbol of the province's maritime heritage. You can find beautifully crafted ship models in various sizes and materials as unique decor pieces or conversation starters.

3. Nova Scotian Cheese and Seafood

Indulge in the flavors of Nova Scotia by bringing home some of its renowned culinary delights. Look for local cheeses and seafood products like smoked salmon, lobster, or Digby scallops, which make for delectable souvenirs or gifts.

4. Handwoven Textiles

Nova Scotia has a strong tradition of textile craftsmanship. Handwoven items such as blankets, scarves, and rugs, often made from local wool, reflect the province's heritage and are both practical and decorative keepsakes.

1. Historic Properties, Halifax

Discover the quaint historic buildings on Halifax's waterfront. There are many boutiques and shops in this region that sell locally manufactured crafts, jewelry, apparel, and artwork. Finding unusual presents is made easy here.

2. Lunenburg

The town of Lunenburg is a UNESCO World Heritage site and a hub for artisan shops. Stroll along the colorful streets and discover boutiques selling everything from pottery and glassware to hand-knit sweaters and jewelry.

3. Wolfville Farmers' Market

If you're in the Annapolis Valley, don't miss the Wolfville Farmers' Market. This bustling market features an array of artisanal products, including local honey, preserves, pottery, and handcrafted soaps.

4. Annapolis Royal

Annapolis Royal, one of Canada's oldest towns, is another treasure trove for artisanal finds. Explore its quaint shops and galleries, where you can purchase pottery, wooden crafts, and artwork inspired by the natural beauty of Nova Scotia.

1. Peggy's Cove Souvenirs

Remember your visit to the iconic Peggy's Cove with a lighthouse-themed souvenir. Look for items like lighthouse-shaped keychains, prints, or hand-painted ornaments.

2. Local Artwork

Nova Scotia has a thriving arts scene. Consider purchasing a piece of local art, such as a painting, sculpture, or photograph, to hang in your home as a beautiful reminder of your trip.

3. Maple Syrup and Maple Products

Nova Scotia is home to sugar maple trees, and you can find high-quality maple syrup and maple products like candies and creams at many local markets and stores.

4. Mi'kmaq Crafts

Support Indigenous artists by purchasing Mi'kmaq crafts, including baskets, beadwork, and jewelry. These items often feature traditional designs and are both culturally significant and beautiful.

Nova Scotia's shopping scene offers a wide range of products that capture the essence of this picturesque province. Whether you're looking for culinary delights, artisanal crafts, or unique souvenirs, you're sure to find the perfect memento to commemorate your Nova Scotian adventure

CHAPTER TWELVE

Practical Information for Nova Scotia Travel

The intriguing location of Nova Scotia, a marine province on Canada's east coast, is renowned for its breathtaking scenery, extensive history, and welcoming people. To guarantee a smooth and pleasurable trip, it's crucial to acquire useful information as you prepare to travel to this picturesque province. We'll go over important topics like money and banking information, as well as health and safety advice for your adventure in Nova Scotia, in this chapter.

Currency and Banking Information

Currency: Canada's official currency is the Canadian Dollar (CAD), represented by the symbol "$" or "C$." It's advisable to exchange some currency before your trip or withdraw CAD from ATMs upon arrival. Credit and debit cards are widely accepted in Nova Scotia, making it convenient for travelers.

Banking Hours: Banks in Nova Scotia generally operate from Monday to Friday, with some branches open on Saturdays. Typical banking hours are from 9:00 AM to 5:00 PM, but this can vary slightly depending on the specific bank and location.

ATMs: You'll find ATMs (Automated Teller Machines) readily available throughout Nova Scotia, especially in urban areas like Halifax, Sydney, and Dartmouth. These

ATMs accept major international credit and debit cards, making it easy to access cash when needed.

Currency Exchange: If you need to exchange foreign currency for Canadian Dollars, banks, currency exchange offices, and some hotels offer this service. However, it's worth noting that exchange rates at airports and hotels may be less favorable than those at banks or dedicated exchange offices.

Health and Safety Tips

Nova Scotia is generally a safe destination for travelers, but it's crucial to take precautions to ensure your well-being during your visit. Here are some health and safety tips to keep in mind:

Travel Insurance: It's advisable to purchase comprehensive travel insurance before your trip. This insurance can cover medical emergencies, trip cancellations, and lost luggage, providing peace of mind during your travels.

Healthcare: Nova Scotia boasts excellent healthcare facilities. If you require medical attention, don't hesitate to visit a hospital or medical clinic. It's also a good idea to carry any necessary prescription medications with you.

Emergency Services: In case of emergencies, dial 911 for immediate assistance. Nova Scotia has a well-established emergency response system.

Weather: Nova Scotia's weather can be unpredictable, so pack accordingly. Layered clothing is a good choice, as it allows you to adapt to changing conditions. Don't forget rain gear, as rain showers are common.

Wildlife: Nova Scotia's natural beauty includes diverse wildlife. If you plan to explore its wilderness, be aware of potential encounters with animals like moose or bears. Follow safety guidelines and maintain a safe distance.

Water Safety: Nova Scotia has many stunning beaches and water activities. When swimming or participating in water sports, be mindful of safety flags, and follow lifeguard instructions.

COVID-19 Precautions: Stay updated on Nova Scotia's COVID-19 guidelines, which may change over time. Adhere to mask mandates, social distancing rules, and vaccination requirements as needed.

Crime: While Nova Scotia is generally safe, exercise common-sense precautions like safeguarding your belongings and being aware of your surroundings, especially in urban areas.

Driving Safety: If you plan to drive in Nova Scotia, familiarize yourself with local traffic laws and road conditions. Be cautious on rural roads, which may have wildlife crossings.

Cultural Respect: Nova Scotians are known for their friendliness. Show respect for local customs, be polite, and enjoy the warm hospitality of the region.

Nova Scotia is a remarkable travel destination offering a blend of natural beauty, history, and culture. By being well-prepared with currency and banking information and following health and safety tips, you can make the most of your Nova Scotia adventure while ensuring a memorable and worry-free experience.

CONCLUSION

Nova Scotia, often referred to as "Canada's Ocean Playground," is a province that leaves an indelible mark on the hearts of both first-time visitors and experienced travelers. This enchanting destination, located on the eastern coast of Canada, is a treasure trove of natural beauty, cultural richness, and historical significance. Whether you're embarking on your first journey to this province or returning to explore its depths further, Nova Scotia offers an array of experiences that captivate the senses and inspire a profound sense of wanderlust.

Natural Wonders: Nova Scotia's stunning landscapes will leave first-time visitors in awe. The dramatic coastline of the Cabot Trail, the rugged beauty of Cape Breton Highlands National Park, and the idyllic charm of Peggy's Cove are just a few of the natural wonders that await. The province's diverse geography, including lush forests, pristine lakes, and picturesque beaches, ensures there's something for every nature enthusiast.

Cultural Immersion: Nova Scotia's rich cultural heritage is deeply rooted in its Acadian, Mi'kmaq, and Scottish influences, among others. First-time visitors can immerse themselves in this cultural tapestry by attending local festivals, visiting heritage sites, and engaging with the friendly locals. Don't forget to try traditional dishes like Digby scallops, seafood chowder, and buttery lobster rolls.

Historical Significance: History buffs will find Nova Scotia a captivating destination. From the historic town of Annapolis Royal, one of North America's oldest European settlements, to the iconic Fortress of Louisbourg, a living history museum, the province's historical sites provide a glimpse into its storied past.

Hospitality: Nova Scotians are renowned for their warm and welcoming nature. First-time visitors will undoubtedly be charmed by the friendliness and helpfulness of the locals. The province's small-town atmosphere fosters a sense of community that makes visitors feel like part of the family.

Outdoor Adventures: Nova Scotia offers a wide range of outdoor activities for the adventurous traveler. Whether it's hiking, kayaking, sailing, or whale-watching along the Bay of Fundy, there's no shortage of thrilling experiences for those seeking an active vacation.

Off the Beaten Path: For those who have already explored Nova Scotia's popular attractions, the province offers numerous off-the-beaten-path gems. Consider venturing to lesser-known areas like Kejimkujik National Park, where you can paddle through serene waterways and camp under a star-studded sky, or the remote Eastern Shore, where you can discover hidden beaches and coastal wilderness.

Culinary Delights: Experienced travelers can dive deeper into Nova Scotia's burgeoning culinary scene. Explore the Annapolis Valley's vineyards and sample award-winning wines, or embark on a seafood trail along the South Shore, savoring the freshest catches of the day at local fishing villages.

Cultural Exchanges: Return visitors can engage more deeply with the local culture, perhaps participating in workshops on Mi'kmaq art or joining traditional ceilidhs (music and dance gatherings). These experiences offer a profound understanding of Nova Scotia's cultural diversity.

Seasonal Exploration: Nova Scotia's beauty changes with the seasons. Experienced travelers might plan their visits to coincide with specific events, such as the vibrant fall foliage, winter's ice wine festivals, or the joyous celebrations of the annual lobster season.

Connect with Nature: Seasoned travelers can take their outdoor adventures to the next level, embarking on multi-day hikes like the Cape Chignecto Coastal Trail or engaging in wildlife conservation programs, contributing to the preservation of Nova Scotia's natural wonders.

Nova Scotia is a destination that continually unfolds its magic to both first-time visitors and experienced travelers. Its unique blend of natural beauty, cultural richness, and historical significance ensures that there is always something new to discover. Whether you're savoring your initial exploration or delving deeper into this captivating province, Nova Scotia's allure remains undeniably irresistible. It's a place where the spirit of adventure thrives, where history whispers through the wind, and where the warmth of the people leaves an indelible mark on your soul. Nova Scotia is, in every sense, a traveler's paradise.

Made in United States
Troutdale, OR
12/17/2023

15982744R00066